◉ HOTHOUSES ◉

FACING PAGES FACING PAGES

NICHOLAS JENKINS
SERIES EDITOR

Horace, The Odes: New Translations
by Contemporary Poets
edited by J. D. McClatchy

Hothouses: Poems 1889
by Maurice Maeterlinck
translated by Richard Howard

HOTHOUSES ◉ POEMS ◉ 1889

Maurice Maeterlinck

Translated by Richard Howard

PRINCETON UNIVERSITY PRESS · PRINCETON AND OXFORD

COPYRIGHT © 2003 BY PRINCETON UNIVERSITY PRESS

PUBLISHED BY PRINCETON UNIVERSITY PRESS, 41 WILLIAM STREET,

PRINCETON, NEW JERSEY 08540

IN THE UNITED KINGDOM: PRINCETON UNIVERSITY PRESS,

3 MARKET PLACE, WOODSTOCK, OXFORDSHIRE OX20 1SY

ISBN: 0-691-08837-3

ISBN (PBK.): 0-691-08838-1

LIBRARY OF CONGRESS CATALOGING-IN-PUBLICATION DATA

MAETERLINCK, MAURICE, 1862–1949.

[SERRES CHAUDES. ENGLISH]

HOTHOUSES / MAURICE MAETERLINCK ; TRANSLATED BY RICHARD HOWARD.

P.   CM.

ISBN 0-691-08837-3 (CL : ALK. PAPER)—ISBN 0-691-08838-1 (PB : ALK. PAPER)

I. HOWARD, RICHARD, 1929– II. TITLE.

PQ2625.A45 S513 2003

841'.8—DC21   2002035698

BRITISH LIBRARY CATALOGING-IN-PUBLICATION DATA IS AVAILABLE

THIS BOOK IS SUPPORTED BY THE CHARLES LACY LOCKERT FUND

OF PRINCETON UNIVERSITY PRESS

ALL WOODCUTS BY GEORGES MINNE, CIRCA 1889. © ARTISTS RIGHTS SOCIETY

(ARS), NEW YORK / SABAM, BRUSSELS. PHOTOGRAPHS © 2003 MUSEUM ASSOCIATES /

LACMA.

THIS BOOK HAS BEEN COMPOSED IN POSTSCRIPT DANTE

PRINTED ON ACID-FREE PAPER. ∞

WWW.PUPRESS.PRINCETON.EDU

PRINTED IN THE UNITED STATES OF AMERICA

1   2   3   4   5   6   7   8   9   10

Contents

Translator's Note

ON MAY 31, 1889, Vanier (Verlaine's publisher) issued in an edition of 155 copies a sequence of 33 poems, 25 in regular, mostly octosyllabic verses, 8 in free verse, a technique already introduced in France by Laforgue and Gustave Kahn but new to Belgium.

The work had been announced as early as 1886 in a "little magazine" of the period, initially as *Les Symboliques*, then as *Les Tentations*, and definitively as *Serres chaudes* [Hothouses], a title that the author, a young lawyer from a wealthy bourgeois family in Ghent, recalled as "a natural choice, Ghent being a horticultural center, abounding in greenhouses and conservatories of all kinds."

To the end of his long life, Maeterlinck was convinced that, as he once wrote to Emile Verhaeren, "there is nothing in the book but Verlaine, Rimbaud, Laforgue, and as people keep telling me, Whitman—almost nothing of myself except perhaps that feeling of things not being where they belong."

Which was just the point, of course. These deviant liturgies take their place in that lineage of French-language poetic alienations (suggestive titles: Baudelaire's *Les Fleurs du mal*, 1857; Hugo's *Les Chatiments*, 1870; Rimbaud's *Une Saison en enfer*, 1873), and indeed *Serres chaudes* forms a hinge between Decadence and a more startling, virtually surreal dislocation which Maeterlinck was to devise in prose (a theater of silence), immediately after he had released these miasmatic exhalations, which figure so guilefully among Modernism's first gasps.

Inveterately, critics have found the formal poems in *Serres chaudes* exasperating. Were they not the very decadence of Decadence, a haggard bloom reluctantly trailing from the *littérature* Verlaine had declared "all the rest" to be, to that still-undetermined *modernisme* exposed by the astonishing "broken imagery" of *vers libre*?

No wonder Max Nordau attacked *Serres chaudes* so greedily in 1892 as instructively degenerate, not perceiving signs of renewal in the uneasy coexistence of convention and innovation: on the one hand those sorrowing lyrics, static and indeed paralyzed, all-too-knowing in their overheated "nursery", and on the other, these disjointed, irrational litanies in turmoil. For us, of course, it is easy enough to see Whitman (the Whitman "people" saw in Maeterlinck) as the antidote to Latin (i.e., French) decadence, not musical but tormented and rhythmically jarring—as Patrick McGuinness, Maeterlinck's best critic, puts it, "an anarchy, but not of freedom and community, but of constriction and isolation."

It was, remarkably, Antonin Artaud who from his uniquely vulnerable position identified the necessarily "creative" energy of this work (in 1924!): "Maeterlinck was the first to introduce the miltiple riches of the subconscious into literature." That insight (however dubious the prioritarian claim) makes it easier for us to realize that the opulent sickliness of these poems leads to the stark minimalism of the one-act plays and of *Pelléas*; we find in both genres the double metaphor of freedom and claustration, of transparency and enclosure, and can acknowledge as only natural the enthusiasm—forgotten nowadays—of those pillars of our incomparable modernity Chekhov and Strindberg, Rilke and Yeats, Mallarmé and Proust.

Certainly Maeterlinck's enormous fame has vanished, though Beckett and William Empson are still among our masters to testify to its significance, its validity. I have added a chronology not to rectify but to establish the record, and have also included, as an appendix to the poems, Maeterlinck's sole "fictive" text, "The Massacre of the Innocents" (1896), based on a Brueghel painting, the better to enable us to follow once again the sinewy trajectory which leads to *Intérieur,* to *Les Aveugles,* and to *Pelléas* from these astonishing nurseries which are *Serres chaudes,* or as we may now call them, *Hothouses.*

RH

Chronology

1862   Maurice Maeterlinck born in Ghent to a French-speaking conservative Catholic family. A vigorous childhood—skating, boating—divided between Ghent and the family estate on a canal connecting Ghent with Terneuzen. Maurice's father, Polydore Maeterlinck, an enthusiastic horticulturalist (a peach named for him).

1867   Preschool at the Sisters of Our Lady, then primary school at the Calamus Institute. A decided interest shown in literary studies.

1874   Enrolled in a Jesuit college where he befriends Charles van Lerberghe, future author of *Bruges-la-Morte*. Joins the school dramatic society.

1881   Studies law at the University of Ghent, respecting a family tradition. Received at the bar four years later. Publishes his first poem, "In the Reeds," under the signature "M. Mater."

1885   Visits Paris. Returns to Ghent and translates into French the Sixteenth-century Flemish mystic Ruysbroeck.

1886   Second visit to Paris, frequenting "advanced" writers, with whom he founds a review, *La Pléiade*, in the third number of which he publishes a tale, "The Massacre of the Innocents," based on a painting by Brueghel, as well as his earliest poems. Meets Villiers de l'Isle-Adam: "the huge admiration, the finest memory, and the great revelation of my life, which divides into two parts, before and after Villiers: on one side darkness, on the other light."

1886–1895	Practices law sporadically. Raises bees, engages in sports, publishes the poems that will constitute the collection *Serres chaudes* [Hothouses].
1889	*Serres chaudes* published with seven woodcuts by Georges Minne, in Paris. Verhaeren declares the work "a turning-point in contemporarty poetry." Publishes first play, *La Princesse Maleine*, in Ghent; Octave Mirbeau (given a copy by Mallarmé) enthusiastically reviews it in *Le Figaro*, comparing the unknown author, not unfavorably, with Shakespeare.
1890	*Les Aveugles* [The Blind] published in Paris, first of a series of one-act plays.
1891	*Les Sept princesses* [The Seven Princesses] published. Maeterlinck publishes his French translation of Ruysbroeck with an introduction. *L'Intruse* [The Intruder] performed in Paris.
1892	*Pelléas et Mélisande* published in Brussels.
1893	*Pelléas et Mélisande* performed in Paris.
1894	Maeterlinck's adaptation [as *Annabella*] of Ford's *'Tis Pity She's a Whore*. Three one-act plays for marionettes—*Alladine et Palomides*, *Intérieur*, and *La Mort de Tintagiles* published. Maeterlinck publishes an introduction to "Seven Essays by Emerson," which he has translated under the name "I. Will."
1895	Maeterlinck meets the actress Georgette Leblanc. Publishes his French translation of works by Novalis with an introduction. Travels in England.
1896	Publishes first collection of philosophical essays, *Le Trésor des humbles* [The Treasure of the Humble]. *Aglavaine et Selysette* performed in Paris. Publishes preface to Mauclair's study of Laforgue. Travels in Italy.
1897	Moves to Paris and to a series of country residences.

1898   Publishes *Sagesse et destinée* [Wisdom and Destiny], second volume of philosophical essays. Travels in Spain.

1899   *Ariane et Barbe-bleu* [Ariadne and Bluebeard] first published in a German translation in Vienna.

1901   *Soeur Béatrice* [Sister Beatrice] first published in a German translation in Berlin. Publishes *La Vie des abeilles* [The Life of the Bee], Maeterlinck's first work to gain a popular audience.

1902   Publishes *Le Temple enseveli* [The Buried Temple], a philosophical essay. Debussy's opera based on *Pelléas et Mélisande* performed in Paris. *Monna Vanna* performed and published.

1903   Polydore Maeterlinck dies. Maurice buys a villa in Grasse. *Joyzelle* performed and published.

1904   *Le Miracle de Saint Antoine* first published in a German translation in Leipzig.

1905   Maeterlinck acquires and moves into Saint-Wandrille, a former Benedictine monastery in western France. Publishes *L'Intelligence des fleurs*, another collection of philosophical essays.

1909   *L'Oiseau bleu* [The Bluebird] first performed by the Moscow Art Theater. Maeterlinck's translation of *Macbeth* performed at Saint-Wandrille.

1910   *Marie-Magdeleine* first performed in a German translation in Leipzig.

1911   Maeterlinck awarded Nobel Prize in Literature. Moves to Nice. Publishes *La Mort*, an essay.

1912   The city of Brussels organizes a gala performance in Maeterlinck's honor in the presence of the royal family, at which Fauré conducts his orchestral interludes for *Pelléas et Mélisande*.

1914	Maeterlinck's attempt to enlist rejected by the Belgian government. *L'Hôte inconnu* [The Unknown Guest], a study of occult sciences, first published in English.
1915	Maeterlinck serves his country by giving a series of lectures in England, Spain, and Italy.
1916	*Le Débris de la guerre* [The War's Debris], an anti-German tract, published.
1918	*Le Bourgmestre de Stilmonde,* a war play, first performed in Buenos Aires. Maeterlinck separates from Georgette Leblanc.
1919	Maeterlinck marries Renée Lahon, buys the Château de Médan. *Les Sentiers de la montagne* [The Mountain Paths] published. Lecture tour of several months in the United States.
1920	The King of Belgium appoints Maeterlinck one of the founders of the Académie Royale de Langue et de Littérature Françaises.
1921	*Le Grand secret* [The Great Secret], an essay, published. Maeterlinck writes an an introduction to the Epistles of Seneca.
1922	*Les Fiançailles* [Engaged].
1925	*Le Malheur passe* [Misfortune Passes].
1926	*La Vie des termites* [The Life of the Termite]. *La Puissance des morts* [The Power of the Dead]. *Berniquel.*
1927	*Marie-Victor. En Sicile et en Calabre* [In Sicily and in Calabria], travel writing.
1928	*La Vie de l'espace* [The Life of Space].
1929	*La Vie des fourmis* [The Life of the Ant]. *L'Araignée de verre* [The Glass Spider]. Maeterlinck buys an estate in Nice, which he names Orlamonde. He is made a count on his seventieth birthday.
1933	*La Grande loi* [The Great Law] published.
1934	*Avant le grand silence* [Before the Great Silence].

1935	*La Princesse Isabelle.*
1936	*Le Sablier* [The Hourglass], essays. *L'Ombre des ailes* [The Shadow of Wings].
1937	*Devant Dieu* [Before God]. Publishes a preface to Olivier Salazar's *A Revolution in Peace.*
1938	*La Grande porte* [The Great Door]. Maeterlinck is in Portugal when war breaks out. He sails for New York, then settles in Palm Beach.
1942	*Le Cadran stellaire* [The Star Dial], essays and aphorisms.
1947	The Maeterlincks return to Orlamonde.
1948	*Jeanne d'Arc. Bulles bleues* [Blue Bubbles], memoirs.
1949	Maeterlinck dies in Nice.

◉ **HOTHOUSES** ◉

Ô serre au milieu des forêts !
Et vos portes à jamais closes !
Et tout ce qu'il y a sous votre coupole !
Et sous mon âme en vos analogies !

Les pensées d'une princesse qui a faim,
L'ennui d'un matelot dans le désert,
Une musique de cuivre aux fenêtres des incurables.

Allez aux angles les plus tièdes !
On dirait une femme évanouie un jour de moisson ;
Il y a des postillons dans la cour de l'hospice ;
Au loin, passe un chasseur d'élans, devenu infirmier.

Examinez au clair de lune !
(Oh rien n'y est à sa place !)
On dirait une folle devant les juges,
Un navire de guerre à pleines voiles sur un canal,
Des oiseaux de nuit sur des lys,
Un glas vers midi,
(Là-bas sous ces cloches !)
Une étape de malades dans la prairie,
Une odeur d'éther un jour de soleil.

Mon Dieu ! mon Dieu ! quand aurons-nous la pluie,
Et la neige et le vent dans la serre !

i ◉ Hothouse

A hothouse deep in the woods,
doors forever sealed. Analogies:
everything under that glass dome,
everything under my soul.

Thoughts of a starving princess,
a sailor marooned in the desert,
fanfares at hospital windows.

Seek out the warmest corners!
Think of a woman fainting on harvest-day;
postillions ride into the hospital courtyard;
a soldier passes, he is a sick-nurse now.

Look at it all by moonlight
(nothing is where it belongs).
Think of a madwoman haled before judges,
a man-of-war in full sail on the canal,
nightbirds perched among the lilies,
a knell at noon
(out there under those glass bell-jars),
cripples halted in the fields
on a day of sunshine, the smell of ether.

My God, when will the rain come,
and the snow, and the wind, to this glass house!

Ayez pitié de mon absence
Au seuil de mes intentions !
Mon âme est pâle d'impuissance
Et de blanches inactions.

Mon âme aux œuvres délaissées,
Mon âme pâle de sanglots
Regarde en vain ses mains lassées
Trembler à fleur de l'inéclos.

Et tandis que mon cœur expire
Les bulles des songes lilas,
Mon âme, aux frêles mains de cire,
Arrose un clair de lune las ;

Un clair de lune où transparaissent
Les lys jaunis des lendemains ;
Un clair de lune où seules naissent
Les ombres tristes de mes mains.

Pity this hesitation of mine
    to speak 'the name of action',
for my soul lies waxen and inert,
    washed transparent

by her own tears, and such indolence
    leaves every task undone:
these helpless hands can only bother
    what they must abort.

And as I watch the lilac bubbles
    rise—O iridescent dreams!—
my soul douses the moon to dimness
    with weary gestures:

yet even that dim moonlight betrays
    tomorrow's yellowed lilies,
revealing no revels but the sad
    shadows of my hands.

Ô cet ennui bleu dans le cœur !
Avec la vision meilleure,
Dans le clair de lune qui pleure,
De mes rêves bleus de langueur !

Cet ennui bleu comme la serre,
Où l'on voit closes à travers
Les vitrages profonds et verts,
Couvertes de lune et de verre,

Les grandes végétations
Dont l'oubli nocturne s'allonge,
Immobilement comme un songe,
Sur les roses des passions ;

Où de l'eau très lente s'élève,
En mêlant la lune et le ciel
En un sanglot glauque éternel,
Monotonement comme un rêve.

O this heart, perpetually blue!
   even with the best vision,
lachrymose by moonlight, of
   my indolent blue dreams;

bored heart, blue as the hothouse
   showing everything blue
through blind glass, slick with moonlight
   and hoarfrost, or is it

only the glass? Suffocating fronds
   by night extend their shadows
motionlessly, as dreams do,
   over passion's roses,

and very slowly the water rises,
   compromising moon and sky
in one endless blue-green sob
   monotonous as dreams.

Ô les glauques tentations
Au milieu des ombres mentales,
Avec leurs flames végétales
Et leurs éjaculations

Obscures de tiges obscures,
Dans le clair de lune du mal,
Eployant l'ombrage automnal
De leurs luxurieux augures !

Elles ont tristement couvert,
Sous leurs muqueuses enlacées
Et leurs fièvres réalisées,
La lune de leur givre vert.

Et leur croissance sacrilège,
Entr'ouvrant ses désirs secrets,
Est morne comme les regrets
Des malades sur de la neige.

Sous les ténèbres de leur deuil,
Je vois s'emmêler les blessures
Des glaives bleus de mes luxures
Dans les chairs rouges de l'orgueil.

Seigneur, les rêves de la terre
Mourront-ils enfin dans mon cœur !
Laissez votre gloire, Seigneur,
Éclairer la mauvaise serre,

Et l'oubli vainement cherché !
Les feuilles mortes de leurs fièvres,
Les étoiles entre leurs lèvres,
Et les entrailles du péché !

O the blind temptations
  amid mental shadows
the fiery blooms of
  these ejaculations

Dark the stems very dark
  by moonlight's malady
but rich the auguries
  of this autumnal hour

Within the slimed embrace
  of their complicit ills
a lichen green as frost
  has sickened the sad moon

Slaking secret desires
  their desecrating growth
is woeful as the woes
  of sick men crossing snow

In the ghosts of their grief
  how many wounds mingle
the blue swords of my lust
  the red flesh of my pride

Lord God let dreams of earth
  die at last in my heart
let your glory my Lord
  clarify this bad glass

The leaves dead of fevers
  and lethe sought in vain
the stars between their lips
  the viscera of sin!

Figure 1. Georges Minne, *Cloches de verre*, circa 1889.

Ô cloches de verre !
Étranges plantes à jamais à l'abri !
Tandis que le vent agite mes sens au dehors !
Toute une vallée de l'âme à jamais immobile !
Et la tiédeur enclose vers midi !
Et les images entrevues à fleur du verre !

N'en soulevez jamais aucune !
On en a mis plusieurs sur d'anciens clairs de lune.
Examinez à travers leurs feuillages :
Il y a peut-être un vagabond sur le trône,
On a l'idée que des corsaires attendent sur l'étang,
Et que des êtres antédiluviens vont envahir les villes.

On en a placé sur d'anciennes neiges.
On en a placé sur de vieilles pluies.
(Ayez pitié de l'atmosphère enclose !)
J'entends célébrer une fête un dimanche de famine,
Il y a une ambulance au milieu de la moisson,
Et toutes les filles du roi errent, un jour de diète, à travers
    les prairies !

Examinez surtout celles de l'horizon !
Elles couvrent avec soin de très anciens orages.
Oh ! Il doit y avoir quelque part une énorme flotte sur un
    marais !
Et je crois que les cygnes ont couvé des corbeaux !
(On entrevoit à peine à travers les moiteurs)

Une vierge arrose d'eau chaude les fougères,
Une troupe de petites filles observe l'ermite en sa cellule,
Mes sœurs sont endormies au fond d'une grotte vénéneuse !

V ◉ GLASS BELL-JARS

Strange plants eternally sheltered
under glass bell-jars
while the wind stirs my senses outdoors!
An entire valley of the soul eternally frozen,
and the heat trapped here by noon—
the image glimpsed on the curve of each bell!

Never lift one of these.
Some have been set on old pools of moonlight;
peer through the foliage:
is that a beggar on the throne?
do pirates lurk on every pond?
are primeval creatures about to invade our cities?

Some have been set on old snowbanks,
some float on stale puddles of rain—
pity that imprisoned air! I hear
people keeping carnival on Hungry Sunday.
An ambulance is parked in the harvest fields,
and on fast-days all the king's daughters wander
across the pastures.

Just look at those on the horizon,
how carefully they mask immemorial storms!
Somewhere there must be a vast armada in the marshes,
and I think the swans have hatched . . . crows!
(it's hard to see in all this wet)
A virgin pours hot water on the ferns,
the hermit in his cell is observed by a troupe of little girls.
Deep in some foul cave my sisters have fallen asleep!

Attendez la lune et l'hiver,
Sur ces cloches éparses enfin sur la glace !

Wait for winter and the moon at last on these bell-jars
  scattered across the ice.

FIGURE 2. Georges Minne, *Offrande obscure*, circa 1889.

J'apporte mon mauvais ouvrage
Analogue aux songes des morts,
Et la lune éclaire l'orage
Sur la faune de mes remords :

Les serpents violets des rêves
Qui s'enlacent dans mon sommeil,
Mes désirs couronnés de glaives,
Des lions noyés au soleil,

Des lys au fond des eaux lointaines
Et des mains closes sans retour,
Et les tiges rouges des haines
Entre les deuils verts de l'amour.

Seigneur, ayez pitié du verbe !
Laissez mes mornes oraisons
Et la lune éparse dans l'herbe
Faucher la nuit aux horizons !

I bring my bad work, analogous
   to the dreams of dead men,
and the moon only adds to the storm
   breaking over the brutes of my remorse:

purple snakes of nightmare castigate
   what passes for my sleep,
all my desires are crowned with drawn swords,
   and lions drowned in nothing but the sun,

lilies drowning too in distant pools;
   hands are forever closed,
and between the red tendrils of hate
   show love's emerald tendrils—widow's weeks!

Lord, take pity on the words of men!
   Let these weary prayers
and a moon disheveled among reeds
   reap the night to the world's farthest rim!

Sous la cloche de cristal bleu
De mes lasses mélancolies,
Mes vagues douleurs abolies
S'immobilisent peu à peu :

Végétations de symboles,
Nénuphars mornes des plaisirs,
Palmes lentes de mes désirs,
Mousses froides, lianes molles.

Seul, un lys érige d'entre eux,
Pâle et rigidement débile,
Son ascension immobile
Sur les feuillages douloureux,

Et dans les lueurs qu'il épanche
Comme une lune, peu à peu,
Élève vers le cristal bleu
Sa mystique prière blanche.

Under the blue bell-jar
   of my listless moods
griefs are suffocated,
   gradually stilled:

'a forest of symbols':
   sleepy lotuses,
soft mosses, slack vines, slow
   pines of my desires . . .

Among these one lily,
   rigid, weak and pale,
rises like a moon above
   the muttering leaves,

and by that luster so
   impassively shed
presses white orisons
   up against the glass.

Ô mes yeux que l'ombre élucide
À travers mes désirs divers,
Et mon cœur aux rêves ouverts,
Et mes nuits dans mon âme humide !

J'ai trempé dans mon esprit bleu
Les roses des attentes mortes ;
Et mes cils ont fermé les portes
Sur des vœux qui n'auront plus lieu.

Mes doigts, aux pâles indolences
Élèvent en vain, chaque soir,
Les cloches vertes de l'espoir
Sur l'herbe mauve des absences.

Et mon âme impuissante a peur
Des songes aigus de ma bouche,
Au milieu des lys que j'attouche ;
Éclipse aux moires de mon cœur ! . . .

O my eyes these shadows manifest,
    falling across each desire,
and my heart enthralled by shadows too—
    miasma within the soul!

I have steeped in blue rumination
    the roses of failed attempts,
and my lashes are closed upon vows
    no longer to be made.

Night after night my indolent hands
    unavailingly set out
the emerald glass bell-jars of hope
    in these forsaken gardens.

And my impotent soul, as I grope
    among the lilies, trembles
with fear of the dreams that choke my breath . . .
    In my faltering heart, eclipse!

Mon âme !
Ô mon âme vraiment trop à l'abri !
Et ces troupeaux de mes désirs dans une serre !
Attendant une tempête sur les prairies !

Allons vers les plus malades :
Ils ont d'étranges exhalaisons.
Au milieu d'eux, je traverse un champ de bataille avec ma
    mère.
On enterre un frère d'armes à midi,
Tandis que les sentinelles prennent leur repas.

Allons aussi vers les plus faibles :
Ils ont d'étranges sueurs ;
Voici une fiancée malade,
Une trahison le dimanche
Et des petits enfants en prison.
(Et plus loin, à travers la vapeur,)
Est-ce une mourante à la porte d'une cuisine ?
Ou une sœur épluchant des légumes au pied du lit d'un
    incurable ?

Allons enfin vers les plus tristes :
(En dernier lieu, car ils ont des poisons.)
Oh ! mes lèvres acceptent les baisers d'un blessé !
Toutes les châtelaines sont mortes de faim, cet été, dans
    les tours de mon âme !

Voici le petit jour qui entre dans la fête !
J'entrevois des brebis le long des quais,
Et il y a une voile aux fenêtres de l'hôspital.

Too sheltered, O my soul,
and these flocks of my desires, under glass!
until the storm breaks over the fields.

Let us seek out the sick, the worst cases—
strange fumes rising,
and among them I cross a field of battle with my mother.
They are burying a brother-in-arms at noon
while the sentries are at mess.

And seek out the weak, the worst cases—
strange sweats glistening,
here is a sick bride
betrayed one Sunday
and little children in prison.
And over there, through the mist,
is that a woman dying at her kitchen door?
Or is it a Sister shelling peas at a sick man's bedside?

Then seek out the saddest
(last of all, for they have poisons):
O my lips, accept the kisses of a wounded man!
And in my soul's castle-keeps this summer
every chatelaine has starved to death.

Dawn breaks on the holiday!
and I glimpse the sheep down on the quays:
there is a sail passing the hospital windows.
It is a long road from my heart to my soul,
and all the sentries are dead at their posts.

Il y a un long chemin de mon cœur à mon âme !
Et toutes les sentinelles sont mortes à leur poste !

Il y eut un jour une pauvre petite fête dans les faubourgs
   de mon âme !
On y fauchait la ciguë un dimanche matin ;
Et toutes les vierges du couvent regardaient passer les
   vaisseaux sur le canal, un jour de jeûne et de soleil.
Tandis que les cygnes souffraient sous un pont vénéneux ;
On émondait les arbres autour de la prison,
On apportait des remèdes une après-midi de Juin,
Et des repas de malades s'étendaient à tous les horizons !

Mon âme !
Et la tristesse de tout cela, mon âme ! et la tristesse de
   tout cela !

One day there was a festival, a poor little celebration
in the suburbs of my soul.
They were cutting down the hemlock one Sunday
    morning;
and all the convent virgins were watching the boats
    passing
on the canal, it was a fast-day, and sunny.
While the swans were choking under a rotting bridge
they were pruning the trees around the prison
and bringing medicine, one afternoon in June,
and meals for the sick were set out everywhere!

O my soul, the sadness of these things,
the sadness of it all!

Ils ne savent plus où se poser ces baisers,
Ces lèvres sur des yeux aveugles et glacés ;
Désormais endormis en leur songe superbe,
Ils regardent rêveurs comme des chiens dans l'herbe,
La foule des brebis grises à l'horizon,
Brouter le clair de lune épars sur le gazon,
Aux caresses du ciel, vague comme leur vie ;
Indifférents et sans une flamme d'envie,
Pour ces roses de joie écloses sous leurs pas ;
Et ce long calme vert qu'ils ne comprennent pas.

X ◉ LASSITUDE

They have forgotten kisses that can make
Cold eyes warm and blind eyes see again;
Henceforth surrendered to complacent dreams,
They torpidly watch, like hounds in tall grass,
The flock of gray lambs on the horizon
Cropping the moonlight spread across a field
Caressed by skies as vague as their own life;
Indifferent and not once envying
The happy roses blooming underfoot—
A long green peace they cannot understand.

Mon âme est malade aujourd'hui,
Mon âme est malade d'absences,
Mon âme a le mal des silences,
Et mes yeux l'éclaircent d'ennui.

J'entrevois d'immobiles chasses,
Sous les fouets bleus des souvenirs,
Et les chiens secrets des désirs,
Passent le long des pistes lasses.

À travers de tièdes forêts,
Je vois les meutes de mes songes,
Et vers les cerfs blancs des mensonges,
Les jaunes flèches des regrets.

Mon Dieu, mes désirs hors d'haleine,
Les tièdes désirs de mes yeux,
Ont voilé de souffles trop bleus
La lune dont mon âme est pleine.

A malady! crammed with absences,
    silences, surely
my soul is a sick soul, and the light
    of my eyes is spent.

All pursuits are paralyzed under
    memory's blue lash,
and the secret hounds of desire
    follow a faint spoor.

In sopping woods, the hunt is met—
    the white stag of lies
efficiently brought down by regret:
    those jaundiced arrows!

Lord, how the tepid lust of my eyes
    and my winded wants
have shrouded with sighs the hunter's moon
    that once lit my soul!

Ô les passions en allées
Et les rires et les sanglots !
Malades et les yeux mi-clos
Parmi les feuilles effeuillées,

Les chiens jaunes de mes péchés,
Les hyènes louches de mes haines,
Et sur l'ennui pâle des plaines
Les lions de l'amour couchés !

En l'impuissance de leur rêve
Et languides sous la langueur
De leur ciel morne et sans couleur,
Elles regarderont sans trêve

Les brebis des tentations
S'éloigner lentes, une à une,
En l'immobile clair de lune,
Mes immobiles passions.

O my passions on the paths,
  laughter, and sobbing!
Ailing, and eyes half-shut
  among fallen leaves,

the yellow hounds of my sins,
  loathing's hyenas,
and on the colorless plains
  love's couchant lions!

In the impotence of their dream
  and languid under the spell
of that lackluster sky, they gaze
  unceasingly, unblinking

at my temptations, so many sheep
  one by one slowly leaving
in the motionless moonlight,
  my motionless passions.

Mon âme a peur comme une femme,
Voyez ce que j'ai fiat, Seigneur,
De mes mains, les lys de mon âme,
De mes yeux, les cieux de mon cœur !

Ayez pitié de mes misères !
J'ai perdu la palme et l'anneau ;
Ayez pitié de mes priéres,
Faibles fleurs dans un verre d'eau.

Ayez pitié du mal des lèvres,
Ayez pitié de mes regrets,
Semez des lys le long des fièvres
Et des roses sur les marais.

Mon Dieu ! d'anciens vols de colombes
Jaunissent le ciel de mes yeux,
Ayez pitié du lin des lombes
Qui m'entoure de gestes bleus !

My soul is scared, womanish:
  Lord, see what I have done
with my hands, the soul's lilies,
  with my eyes, the heart's sky!

Take pity on my despairs!
  I have lost palm and ring;
take pity on my prayers,
  frail flowers in a glass.

Take pity on these sick lips,
  pity on my regrets;
among fevers strew lilies,
  on the quagmires roses.

My God! ancient flights of doves
  jaundice my horizon:
take pity on the loincloths
  folding me in blue signs!

Voici d'anciens désirs qui passent,
Encor des songes de lassés,
Encor des rêves qui se lassent ;
Voilà les jours d'espoir passés !

En qui faut-il fuir aujourd'hui !
Il n'y a plus d'étoile aucune :
Mais de la glace sur l'ennui
Et des linges bleus sous la lune.

Encor des sanglots pris au piège !
Voyez les malades sans feu,
Et les agneaux brouter la neige ;
Ayez pitié de tout, mon Dieu !

Moi, j'attends un peu de réveil,
Moi, j'attends que le sommeil passe,
Moi, j'attends un peu de soleil
Sur mes mains que la lune glace.

Old desires are fading now,
The dreams of tired men and
Even tired dreams. The days
Of hope are past hoping for.

What asylum on such a day?
Not a single star remains;
Only boredom in its icy caul
And linens blue by moonlight.

Ever more laments ensnared.
See those sick men in the dark,
And the lambs cropping snow.
Lord, have pity on us all!

I wait for a little waking,
I wait for sleep to be over.
I wait for a little sunshine
On my moon-chapped hands.

Les paons nonchalants, les paons blancs ont fui,
Les paons blancs ont fui l'ennui du réveil ;
Je vois les paons blancs, les paons d'aujourd'hui,
Les paons en allés pendant mon sommeil,
Les paons nonchalants, les paons d'aujourd'hui,
Atteindre indolents l'étang sans soleil,
J'entends les paons blancs, les paons de l'ennui,
Attendre indolents les temps sans soleil.

XV ◉ TEDIUM

Listless, the white peacocks are gone,
they have fled waking's tedium; yet
I see them, today's white peacocks
gone while I slept, white peacocks
indolently seeking a sunless pool,
I hear the white peacocks of tedium
indolently awaiting sunless days.

FIGURE 3. Georges Minne, *Hôpital*, circa 1889.

Hôpital ! hôpital au bord du canal !
Hôpital au mois de Juillet !
On y fait du feu dans la salle !
Tandis que les transatlantiques sifflent sur le canal !

(Oh ! n'approchez pas des fenêtres !)
Des émigrants traversent un palais !
Je vois un yacht sous la tempête !
Je vois des troupeaux sur tous les navires !
(Il vaux mieux que les fenêtres restent closes,
On est presque à l'abri du dehors.)
On a l'idée d'une serre sur la neige,
On croit célébrer des relevailles un jour d'orage,
On entrevoit des plantes éparses sur une couverture de
    laine,
Il y a un incendie un jour de soleil,
Et je traverse une forêt pleine de blessés.

Oh ! voice enfin le clair de lune !

Un jet d'eau s'élève au milieu de la salle !
Une troupe de petites filles entr'ouvre la porte !
J'entrevois des agneaux dans une île de prairies !
Et de belles plantes sur un glacier !
Et des lys dans un vestibule de marbre !
Il y a un festin dans une forêt vierge !
Et une végétation orientale dans une grotte de glace !

Écoutez ! on ouvre les écluses !
Et les transatlantiques agitent l'eau du canal !

Voyez la sœur de charité qui attise le feu !

It is right on the bank of the canal,
and even in July fires are lit in the wards.
You can even hear the steamships
hooting out on the canal.

(Oh! keep away from the windows!)
Refugees are swarming through the palace.
I see a yacht out in the storm
and herds of cattle on all the barges.
(Better keep the windows shut,
we're likely to be safe here.)
It's as if there's a hothouse in the snow,
and a woman being churched on a stormy day.
You can make out ferns
scattered on a woolen counterpane.

A fire has broken out on a sunny day
and the woods I'm walking through
are full of wounded men.

There's the moonlight, finally!

A fountain bubbles up in the middle of the ward.
There are lilies in a marble lobby.
A troupe of little girls peers around the door
they have just opened.

I can see lambs on that island—they're in the meadow,
and splendid vines growing on a glacier!

A banquet is being served in a virgin forest,
and there are exotic plants in a cave of ice!

Tous les beaux roseaux verts des berges sont en flamme !
Un bateau de blessés ballotte au clair de lune !
Toutes les filles du roi sont dans une barque sous l'orage !
Et les princesses vont mourir en un champ de ciguës !

Oh ! n'entrouvrez pas les fenêtres !
Écoutez : les transatlantiques sifflent encore à l'horizon !

On empoisonne quelqu'un dans un jardin !
Ils célèbrent une grande fête chez les ennemis !
Il y a des cerfs dans une ville assiégée !
Et une ménagerie au milieu des lys !
Il y a une végétation tropicale au fond d'une houillère !
Un troupeau de brebis traverse un pont de fer !
Et les agneaux de la prairie entrent tristement dans la
      salle !

Maintenant la sœur de charité allume les lampes,
Elle apporte le repas des malades,
Elle a clos les fenêtres sur le canal,
Et toutes les portes au clair de lune.

Hear that? The locks are being opened,
and the liners are making huge waves
on the usually still waters of the canal.

Look! the Sister is stoking the fire now.

All the tall green reeds on the bank are blazing!
A ship carrying the wounded tosses in the moonlight.

Every one of the king's daughters is in that boat
out in the storm!
And the princesses will die in groves of hemlock.

No, don't open the windows!
Listen, the steamers are still hooting on the horizon.

Someone is being poisoned in a garden,
And our enemies are celebrating a momentous festival!
Stags have broken into a besieged village,
and there is a zoo of sorts among the lilies!

Look! At the bottom of a coal-pit, a clump
of tropical vegetation!
A flock of sheep is crossing an iron bridge,
and the lambs from the meadow—how sad they look!
are coming into the ward.

Now the Sister is lighting the lamps
and serving the patients their meals.
She has closed the windows on the canal side
and every door that lets in moonlight.

En mes oraisons endormies
Sous de languides visions,
J'entends jaillir les passions
Et des luxuries ennemies.

Je vois un clair de lune amer
Sous l'ennui nocturne des rêves ;
Et sur de vénéneuses grèves,
La joie errante de la chair.

J'entends s'élever dans mes moelles
Des désirs aux horizons verts,
Et sous des cieux toujours couverts,
Je souffre une soif sans étoiles !

J'entends jaillir dans ma raison
Les mauvaises tendresses noires ;
Je vois des marais illusoires
Sous une éclipse à l'horizon !

Et je meurs sous votre rancune !
Seigneur, ayez pitié, Seigneur,
Ouvrez au malade en sueur
L'herbe entrevue au clair de lune !

Il est temps, Seigneur, il est temps
De faucher la ciguë inculte !
À travers mon espoir occulte
La lune est verte de serpents !

Et le mal des songes afflue
Avec ses péchés en mes yeux,
Et j'écoute des jets d'eau bleus
Jaillir vers la lune absolue !

In my somnolent prayers
after languid visions,
I feel the passions stirring—
lecheries hostile to me.

Bitter the moonlight I see
through my dreams' tedium;
and on a villainous shore
the errant joys of flesh.

In my veins the longings start
for their green horizons,
and beneath overcast skies
I suffer a starless thirst!

I feel them mount in my mind,
the bad black desires,
and beneath a far eclipse
I see the misleading marshes.

Thy rancor kills, O Lord,
Have pity on my dying;
grant to a fevered thirst
those sublunar meadows . . .

Despite my shrouded hopes,
the moon is green with snakes.
It is time, Lord, it is time
to reap the wild hemlock,

for the pestilence of dreams
imbues my eyes with sin,
and blue fountains—I hear them!
spurt to the absolute moon!

FIGURE 4. Georges Minne, *Désirs d'hiver*, circa 1889.

Je pleure les lèvres fanées
Où les baisers ne sont pas nés,
Et les désirs abandonnés
Sous les tristesses moissonnées.

Toujours la pluie à l'horizon !
Toujours la neige sur les grèves !
Tandis qu'au seuil clos de mes rêves,
Des loups couchés sur le gazon,

Observent en mon âme lasse,
Les yeux ternis dans le passé,
Tout le sang autrefois versé
Des agneaux mourants sur la glace.

Seule la lune éclaire enfin
De sa tristesse monotone,
Où gèle l'herbe de l'automne,
Mes désirs malades de faim.

Where kisses no longer glow
    I mourn the faded lips,
the hungers now resigned
    to melancholy gleanings.

Endless the sopping fields,
    endless the icy beaches!
Wolves sprawled in the grass
    on the verge of my dreams

stare with faltering eyes
    at my weary soul's spoils:
all that squandered blood
    of dead lambs in the snow;

and under its despondent glare
    that withers the autumn reeds
only the moon betrays
    the famine of my desire.

Je chante les pâles ballades
Des baisers perdus sans retour !
Sur l'herbe épaisse de l'amour
Je vois des noces de malades.

J'entends des voix dans mon sommeil
Si nonchalamment apparues !
Et des lys s'ouvrent en des rues
Sans étoiles et sans soleil.

Et ces élans si lents encore
Et ces désirs que je voulais,
Sont des pauvres dans un palais,
Et des cierges las dans l'aurore.

J'attends la lune dans mes yeux
Ouverts au seuil des nuits sans trêves,
Afin qu'elle étanche mes rêves
Avec ses linges lents et bleus.

On love's rich lawns
I watch the cripples' wedding,
singing the pale refrains
of kisses lost forever.

I hear the listless voices
in my sleep. And lilies
bloom, opening in streets
without stars, without sun.

All these faltering forces,
desperate longings! like
vagabonds in a palace,
or candles weak at dawn.

My eyes await a moon
on the brink of endless nights—
let my dreams be smothered
in these slow blue sheets!

Il est l'heure enfin de bénir
Le sommeil éteint des esclaves,
Et j'attends ses mains à venir
En roses blanches dans les caves.

J'attends enfin son souffle frais,
Sur mon cœur enfin clos aux fraudes ;
Agneau-pascal dans les marais,
Et blessure au fond des eaux chaudes.

J'attends des nuits sans lendemains,
Et des faiblesses sans remède ;
J'attends son ombre sur mes mains,
Et son image dans l'eau tiède.

J'attends vos nuits afin de voir
Mes désirs se laver la face,
Et mes songes aux bains du soir,
Mourir en un palais de glace.

It is time now for blessing
    the ruined sleep of slaves,
and I wait for hands to come—
    white roses underground.

I wait now for that cool breath
    on my obdurate heart;
paschal-lamb in the marshes,
    a wound in the hot springs.

I wait now for absolute nights
    and hopeless weakness,
I wait for that shadow on my hands,
    that image in the swamp . . .

I wait for those nights so as to see
    my desires washed clean, my dreams
bathed in darkness dying now
    in a palace of ice.

Ô plongeur à jamais sous sa cloche !
Toute une mer de verre éternellement chaude !
Toute une vie immobile aux lents pendules verts !
Et tant d'êtres éstranges à travers les parois !
Et tout attouchement à jamais interdit !
Lorsqu'il y a tant de vie en l'eau claire au dehors !

Attention ! l'ombre des grands voiliers passé sur les
     dahlias des forêts sous-marines ;
Et je suis un moment à l'ombre des baleines qui s'en vont
     vers le pôle !

En ce moment, les autres déchargent, sans doute, des
     vaisseaux pleins de neige dans le port !
Il y avait encore un glacier au milieu des prairies de Juillet !
Ils nagent à reculons en l'eau verte de l'anse !
Ils entrent à midi dans des grottes obscures !
Et les brises du large éventent les terrasses !

Attention ! voici les langues en flamme du Gulf-Stream !
Écartez leurs baisers des parois de l'ennui !
On n'a plus mis de neige sur le front des fiévreux ;
Les malades ont allumé un feu de joie,
Et jettent à pleines mains les lys verts dans les flammes !

Appuyez votre front aux parois les moins chaudes,
En attendant la lune au sommet de la cloche,
Et fermez bien vos yeux aux forêts de pendules bleus et
     d'albumines violettes, en restant sourd aux suggestions
     de l'eau tiède.

O diver forever under his bell,
the whole transparent sea forever warm,
the whole of life motionless in those slow green periods,
    all contact forbidden
with such strange creatures on the other side of the glass,
with so much alive out there in the bright water!

Look how the shadows of great ships pass
    over the dahlias of undersea groves,
and for a moment I too stand in the shadow
    of whales making for the Pole!

In the harbor even now, men must be
    unloading cargoes of ice.
A glacier still remained in the midsummer fields!
They are swimming in the cove's green waters,
    penetrating even the darkest caverns,
    and at noon, offshore winds
    refresh the terraces, each and every one!

Take care, those are the Gulf Stream's fiery tongues—
    keep their kisses away from the idle glass!
Yet snow is no longer laid on a fevered brow
and the sick themselves have lit a bonfire,
    throwing handfuls of green lilies into the flames!

Press your forehead against the coolest part of the glass
    till the moon touches the top of the bell,
and close your eyes to the chromatic forests,
    swaying blues, cloudy purples; your ears
    to the insinuations of tepid water.

Essuyez vos désirs affaiblis de sueures ;
Allez d'abord à ceux qui vont s'évanouir :
Ils ont l'air de célébrer une fête nuptiale dans une cave ;
Ils ont l'air d'entrer à midi, dans une avenue éclairée de
     lampes au fond d'un souterrain ;
Ils traversent, en cortège de fête, un paysage semblable à
     une enfance d'orphelin.

Allez ensuite à ceux qui vont mourir.
Ils arrivent comme des vierges qui ont fait une longue
     promenade au soleil, un jour de jeûne ;
Ils sont pâles comme des malades qui écoutent pleuvoir
     placidement sur les jardins de l'hôpital ;
Ils ont l'aspect de survivants qui déjeunent sur le champ
     de bataille.
Ils sont pareils à des prisonniers qui n'ignorent pas que
     tous les geôliers se baignent dans le fleuve,
Et qui entendent faucher l'herbe dans le jardin de la
     prison.

Wipe your desires dry, weakened with sweat as they are.
Tend first to those about to faint:
    they look as if
they were celebrating a wedding in a dungeon;
    they look as if
they had turned at noon into a lamplit avenue
    underground;
the festive procession is crossing a landscape
    reminiscent of an orphan's childhood.

Then go to those about to die:
they move like virgins who have walked a long way
    in the sun on a day of fasting;
they are pale as the sick who listen patiently
    to the rain in the hospital garden;
they have the look of survivors
    picnicking on the battlefields,
or of prisoners aware that all their jailors have gone
    swimming in the river,
and who hear the grass being mown in the prison garden.

Hélas ! mes vœux n'amènent plus
Mon âme aux rives des paupières,
Elle est descendue au reflux
   De ses prières.

Elle est au fond de mes yeux clos,
Et seule son haleine lasse
Élève encore à fleur des eaux
   Ses lys de glace.

Ses lèvres au fond des douleurs,
Semblent closes à mille lieues,
Et je les vois chanter des fleurs
   A tiges bleues.

Ses doigts blanchissent mes regards,
En suivant la trace incolore
De ses lys à jamais épars
   Et morts d'éclore.

Et je sais qu'elle doit mourir
En joignant ses mains impuissantes,
Et lasses enfin de cueillir
   Ces fleurs absentes.

Desires no longer draw my soul
to the sill of vision; she has sunk
submissive to the ceaseless ebb-
    tide of her prayers.

Behind my tight-shut lids she lies,
and only her weary breath can still
raise to the water's surface her
    lotuses of ice.

In depths of pain her lips seem sealed
a world away, yet I see them stir,
singing in praise of water-lilies
    lolling on blue stems.

Her fingers blind my eyes as I
follow the transparent spoor
of such lilies' ever-scattered clumps,
    dying of blooming.

And I know that she will have to die,
folding her helpless hands that are
finally tired of gathering up
    those absent flowers.

Je regarde d'anciennes heures,
Sous le verre ardent des regrets ;
Et du fond bleu de leurs secrets
Émergent des flores meilleures.

Ô ce verre sur mes désirs !
Mes désirs à travers mon âme !
Et l'herbe morte qu'elle enflamme
En approchant des souvenirs !

Je l'élève sur mes pensées,
Et je vois éclore au milieu
De la fuite du cristal bleu,
Les feuilles des douleurs passées.

Jusqu'à l'éloignement des soirs
Morts si longtemps en ma mémoire,
Qu'ils troublent de leur lente moire
L'âme verte d'autres espoirs.

When I gaze at bygone days
through the burning-glass of regret,
    strange flowers are ignited
from the blue ash of their mysteries.

Through the glass, my desires!
My desires through the lens of my soul!
    and at memory's approach
even the dead grass bursts into flame!

I hold the glass to my thoughts
and see in that crystal labyrinth
    the petals of old pain bloom
as if they were not things of the past . . .

I see those faraway nights
so long dead to memory that their
    gradually focused return
withers the green soul of hopes to come.

Sous l'eau du songe qui s'élève,
Mon âme a peur, mon âme a peur !
Et la lune luit dans mon cœur,
Plongé dans les sources du rêve.

Sous l'ennui morne des roseaux,
Seuls les reflets profonds des choses,
Des lys, des palmes et des roses,
Pleurent encore au fond des eaux.

Les fleurs s'effeuillent une à une
Sur le reflet du firmament,
Pour descendre éternellement
Dans l'eau du songe et dans la lune.

Under the rising tide of dreams, my soul
　　is suddenly afraid,
for in my heart a ruthless moon shows where
　　all such dreaming begins:

under the sullen sameness of the reeds,
　　only the reflections
of palms, lilies, roses—all upside down—
　　weep into the waters.

One by one the flowers drop their petals
　　on the sky's reflection,
sinking eternally into the mirror
　　of dreams, into the moon!

Je vois passer tous mes baisers,
Toutes mes larmes dépensées ;
Je vois passer dans mes pensées
Tous mes baisers désabusés.

C'est des fleurs sans couleur aucune,
Des jets d'eau bleus à l'horizon,
De la lune sur le gazon,
Et des lys fanés dans la lune.

Lasses et lourdes de sommeil,
Je vois sous mes paupières closes,
Les corbeaux au milieu des roses,
Et les malades au soleil,

Et lent sur mon âme indolente,
L'ennui de ces vagues amours
Luire immobile et pour toujours,
Comme une étoile pâle et lente.

XXV ◉ VISIONS

I see them all, the kisses, the tears,
    shed and obsolete;
I see them all vanish into my
    disillusioned dreams.

As if by moonlight, these gardens are
    colorless, the fountains
blue in the distance, the new lilies
    already withered.

Listless, sleep-heavy, my closing lids
    nonetheless reveal
crows among the roses, sick men
    taking the sun, and

on my languid soul falls the tedium
    of those vague loves
shining as inert and eternal
    as some pale star.

Vous savez, Seigneur, ma misère !
Voyez ce que je vous apporte !
Des fleurs mauvaises de la terre,
Et du soleil sur une morte.

Voyez aussi ma lassitude,
La lune éteinte et l'aube noire ;
Et fécondez ma solitude
En l'arrosant de votre gloire.

Ouvrez-moi, Seigneur, votre voie,
Éclairez-y mon âme lasse,
Car la tristesse de ma joie
Semble de l'herbe sous la glace.

xxvi ◉ PRAYER

Lord, you know my wretchedness,
   you see what I bring you:
baneful flowers of the earth,
   sun on a woman's corpse.

My torpor too you see, the moon
   missing and the dawn black;
send me the rain of your glory, Lord,
   make my wasteland bloom.

Show me the way, Lord, and shed
   light on my dim soul,
for so grievous is my joy it seems
   but grass beneath the ice.

Ô ces regards pauvres et las !
Et les vôtres et les miens !
Et ceux qui ne sont plus et ceux qui vont venir !
Et ceux qui n'arriveront jamais et qui existent cependant !
Il y en a qui semblent visiter des pauvres un dimanche;
Il y en a comme des malades sans maison ;
Il y en a comme des agneaux dans une prairie couverte
    de linges.
Et ces regards insolites !
Il y en a sous la voûte desquels on assiste à l'exécution
    d'une vierge dans une salle close,
Et ceux qui font songer à des tristesses ignorées !
À des paysans aux fenêtres de l'usine,
À un jardinier devenu tisserand,
À une après-midi d'été dans un musée de cires,
Aux idées d'une reine qui regarde un malade dans le
    jardin,
À une odeur de camphre dans la forêt,
À enfermer une princesse dans une tour, un jour de fête,
À naviguer toute une semaine sur un canal tiède.
Ayez pitié de ceux qui sortent à petits pas comme des
    convalescents dans la moisson !
Ayez pitié de ceux qui ont l'air d'enfants égarés à l'heure
    du repas !
Ayez pitié des regards du blessé vers le chirurgien,
Pareils à des tentes sous l'orage !
Ayez pitié des regards de la vierge tentée !
(Oh ! des fleuves de lait ont fui dans les ténèbres !
Et les cygnes sont morts au milieu des serpents !)

O those poor tired glances, yours and mine both!
Glances past and to come,
   those which never come and still exist.
Glances that seem to visit the poor on Sundays;
   glances like homeless invalids;
   glances like lambs in a meadow spread with bleaching
     linen.
And those unexpected glances!
Under the vaults of these we witness a virgin being put
   to death in a sealed chamber.
And these make us dream of unknown sorrows:
   of farmers at factory windows,
   of gardeners now laboring as weavers,
   of summer afternoons in a wax museum,
   of a queen's thoughts on seeing a sick man in the
     garden,
   of the smell of camphor in the woods,
   of a princess locked in a tower on a feast-day,
   of a week's navigation on a stagnant canal.
Pity for those who creep out like convalescents at
   harvest-time,
   for those who look like lost children at dinner-time,
   for the wounded man's glances at the surgeon, like
     tents in a storm!
Pity for glances of a virgin tempted (Oh, rivers of milk
   that have trickled into the dark, and the swans dead
   among a nest of snakes)!
And pity too for the virgin who succumbs! The princess
   abandoned in a pathless swamp, and in whose eyes
   you can follow ships sailing away, all lit up in a storm!

Et de ceux de la vierge qui succombe !

Princesses abandonnées en des marécages sans issues ;

Et ces yeux où s'éloignent à pleines voiles des navires
illuminés dans la tempête !

Et le pitoyable de tous ces regards qui souffrent de n'être
pas ailleurs !

Et tant de souffrances presque indistinctes et si diverses
cependant !

Et ceux que nul ne comprendra jamais !

Et ces pauvres regards presque muets !

Et ces pauvres regards qui chuchotent !

Et ces pauvres regards étouffés !

Au milieu des uns on croit être dans un château qui sert
d'hôpital !

Et tant d'autres ont l'air de tentes, lys des guerres, sur la
petite pelouse du couvent !

Et tant d'autres ont l'air de blessés soignés dans une serre
chaude !

Et tant d'autres ont l'air de sœurs de charité sur un
Atlantique sans malades !

Oh ! avoir vu tous ces regards !

Avoir admis tous ces regards !

Et avoir épuisé les miens à leur rencontre !

Et désormais ne pouvoir plus fermer les yeux !

Pity for glances which suffer for not being somewhere
   else, for so much suffering so vague and yet so various!
And for those no one will understand, for those virtually
   mute whispering glances, for the poor stifled glances!
With some of these, you might be in a castle being used
   as
   a hospital, while others look like tents, war-lilies
   on the little convent lawn, many others like the
   wounded
   being cared for in a hothouse, and still others like
   sisters of charity on a hospital-ship without patients.

Oh to have met all these glances, to have acknowledged
   them,
   to have exhausted my own in the meeting, and
   henceforth
   to be unable to close my eyes!

Mon âme a joint ses mains étranges
À l'horizon de mes regards ;
Exaucez mes rêves épars
Entre les lèvres de vos anges !

En attendant sous mes yeux las,
Et sa bouche ouverte aux prières
Éteintes entre mes paupières
Et dont les lys n'éclosent pas ;

Elle apaise au fond de mes songes,
Ses seins effeuillés sous mes cils,
Et ses yeux clignent aux périls
Éveillés au fil des mensonges.

My soul has joined her hands, a stranger's hands
　　at the horizon of my gaze;
　　　fulfill these scattered dreams of mine,
Lord God, between your angels' speaking lips!

My soul awaits, beneath depleted eyes
　　and her mouth parted in a prayer
　　　vanished from my vision—those are
ruined lilies: such buds will never open;

My soul seeks peace, sinking into my dreams,
　　her breasts leafless before me,
　　　her eyelids fluttering at the risks
Awakened at the brink of all my lies.

Mes yeux ont pris mon âme au piège,
Mon Dieu, laissez tomber, mon Dieu,
Un peu de feuilles sur la neige,
Un peu de neige sur le feu !

J'ai du soleil sur l'oreiller,
Toujours les mêmes heures sonnent ;
Et mes regards vont s'effeuiller
Sur des mourantes qui moissonnent . . .

Mes mains cueillent de l'herbe sèche,
Et mes yeux ternis de sommeil
Sont des malades sans eau fraîche,
Et des fleurs de cave au soleil.

J'attends de l'eau sur le gazon
Et sur mes songes immobiles,
Et mes regards à l'horizon
Suivent des agneaux dans les villes.

xxix ◉ Afternoon

My eyes have ensnared my soul; I am caught . . .
   Lord, drop some leaves on the snow,
      some snow on the fire!

The sun plays on my pillow; the same hours
   keep chiming, and I can see
      that women gleaning

in the fields are dying. I glean with them—
   nothing but withered grass! and
      my sleep-dimmed eyes

are like sick men without water, as if
   cellar-grown flowers were brought
      out into sunlight.

I wait for rain to waken the fields
   and fall on my unchanging
      dreams, but whenever

I glance at the horizon, I follow
   the flock of lambs heading straight
      for the slaughterhouse.

Je vois des songes dans mes yeux ;
Et mon âme enclose sous verre,
Éclairant sa mobile serre,
Affleure les vitrages bleus.

Ô les serres de l'âme tiède,
Les lys contre les verres clos,
Les roseaux éclos sous leurs eaux,
Et tous mes désirs sans remède !

Je voudrais atteindre, à travers
L'oubli de mes pupilles closes,
Les ombelles autrefois roses
De tous mes songes entr'ouverts . . .

J'attends pour voir leurs feuilles mortes
Reverdir un peu dans mes yeux,
J'attends que la lune aux doigts bleus
Entr'ouvre en silence les portes.

Dreams substitute for what is seen, and
in its luminous prison, my soul
   takes an azure turn.

Under glass the lilies are tepid,
under water the lotuses raise
   an incurable thirst!

Oblivious, I would still pursue
the cavernous once-pink corollas
   of my fantasies . . .

O to see those dead fronds green again,
and the silent fingers of the moon
   set open the gates!

Ayez pitié des yeux moroses
Où l'âme entr'ouvre ses espoirs,
Ayez pitié des inécloses
Et de l'attente au bord des soirs !

Émois des eaux spirituelles !
Et lys mobiles sous leurs flots
Au fil de moires éternelles ;
Et ces vertus sous mes yeux clos !

Mon Dieu, mon Dieu, des fleurs étranges
Montent aux cols des nénuphars ;
Et les vagues mains de vos anges
Agitent l'eau de mes regards.

Et leurs fleurs s'éveillent aux signes
Épars au milieu des flots bleus ;
Et mon âme ouvre au vol des cygnes
Les blanches ailes de mes yeux.

Pity, Lord, these sullen eyes
   where the soul's hopes hide;
pity too the cankered buds
   and the long wait for darkness.

Ripples in the spirit's rill
   stir the drifting lilies
as their listless patterns shift—
   O lights behind closed lids!

Lord, what are these vines
   that choke the lotus stems?
An angel's tentative hands
   dim the visionary tide.

What flowers awake to signs
   blazoned on these waves?
Swans mount! my soul unfolds
   her white wings: I see!

Ô les attouchements !
L'obscurité s'étend entre vos doigts !
Musiques de cuivres sous l'orage !
Musiques d'orgues au soleil !
Tous les troupeaux de l'âme au fond d'une nuit d'éclipse !
Tout le sel de la mer en herbe des prairies !
Et ces bolides bleus à tous les horizons !
(Ayez pitié de ce pouvoir de l'homme !)

Mais ces attouchements plus mornes et plus las !
Ô ces attouchements de vos pauvres mains moites !
J'écoute vos doigts purs passer entre mes doigts,
Et des troupeaux d'agneaux s'éloignent au clair de lune le
    long d'un fleuve tiède.

Je me souviens de toutes les mains qui ont touché mes
    mains.
Et je revois ce qu'il y avait à l'abri de ces mains,
Et je vois aujourd'hui ce que j'étais à l'abri de ces mains
    tièdes.
Je devenais souvent le pauvre qui mange du pain au pied
    du trône.
J'étais parfois le plongeur qui ne peut plus s'évader de
    l'eau chaude !
J'étais parfois tout un peuple qui ne pouvait plus sortir
    des faubourgs !
Et ces mains semblables à un couvent sans jardin !
Et celles qui m'enfermaient comme une troupe de
    malades dans une serre un jour de pluie !
Jusqu'à ce que d'autres plus fraîches vinssent entr'ouvrir
    les portes,
Et répandre un peu d'eau sur le seuil !

O these contacts!
Darkness spreads between your fingers,
the storm's brazen music and the sunshine's
    music too, spreading!
The soul's flocks during the moon's eclipse,
sea-salt crystallizing in the fields,
and blue thunderbolts on every horizon
(take pity on this human power)!

But these sadder contacts, wearier ones!
O these contacts of your poor moist hands—
I hear your pure fingers as they pass between mine,
flocks of lambs moving along the banks
    of a tepid stream by moonlight.

I remember all the hands which ever touched mine,
and I see anew all that was protected
    from those hands,
and today I see what I myself was, protected
    from those hands!
How often I became a pauper gnawing a crust
    at the foot of the throne,
and sometimes I was a diver who can no longer
    escape seething waters,
sometimes I was a whole populace who can no longer
    escape narrow streets!
O those hands, like a convent with no garden!
and hands which confined me, like a host of invalids
in a hothouse on a rainy day
until other, cooler hands came to open the doors,
to sprinkle a little water on the threshold!

Oh ! j'ai connu d'étranges attouchements !
Et voici qu'ils m'entourent à jamais !

On y faisait l'aumône un jour de soleil,
On y faisait la moisson au fond d'un souterrain,
Il y avait une musique de saltimbanques autour de la
    prison,
Il y avait des figures de cire dans une forêt d'été,
Ailleurs la lune avait fauché toute l'oasis,
Et parfois je trouvais une vierge en sueur au fond d'une
    grotte de glace.

Ayez pitié des mains étranges !
Ces mains contiennent les secrets de tous les rois !

Ayez pitié des mains trop pâles !
Elles semblent sortir des caves de la lune,
Elles se sont usées à filer le fuseau des jets d'eau !

Ayez pitié des mains trop blanches et trop moites !
Il me semble que les princesses sont allées se coucher
    vers midi tout l'été !

Éloignez-vous des mains trop dures !
Elles semblent sortir des rochers !
Mais ayez pitié des mains froides !
Je vois un cœur saigner sous des côtes de glace !
Ayez pitié des mains mauvaises !
Elles ont empoisonné les fontaines !
Elles ont mis les jeunes cygnes dans un nid de ciguë !
J'ai vu les mauvais anges ouvrir les portes à midi !
Il n'y a que des fous sur un fleuve vénéneux !
Il n'y a plus que des brebis noires en des pâturages sans
    étoiles !
Et les agneaux s'en vont brouter l'obscurité !

Certainly I have known strange contacts,
and they are here around me forever!

Some would give alms on a day when the sun shone,
and some would harvest what grew in the cellar,
and tumblers would be singing around the prison,
there would be waxwork figures in the woods
    all summer long,
though elsewhere the moon had mown the whole oasis,
and sometimes, deep in a cave of ice, I would find
    a virgin covered with sweat.

Take pity on these strange hands,
these hands which hold the secrets of so many kings!

Take pity on hands which are too pale,
which seem to emerge from the caverns of the moon,
hands worn by unwinding threads from the spindles
    of the fountain!

Take pity on hands which are too white, too moist!
I believe the princesses have gone to bed at midday
    all summer long!

Avoid hands which are too hard,
they seem to have crept out of the rocks!
But take pity on these cold hands,
for I see a heart bleeding under ribs of ice!
Take pity on these wicked hands:
they have poisoned the springs,
they have put the cygnets in a nest of hemlock!
I have seen the angels of evil open the gates at noon,
and now there are only madmen on a pestilent river,
there are only black lambs in the starless pastures,
and the lambs move off, cropping the darkness.

Mais ces mains fraîches et loyales !
Elles viennent offrir des fruits mûrs aux mourants !
Elles apportent de l'eau claire et froide en leurs paumes !
Elles arrosent de lait les champs de bataille !
Elles semblent sortir d'admirables forêts éternellement
   vierges !

But these cool and faithful hands!
They come offering ripe fruits to the dying,
they bring clear cold water in their palms,
they moisten the battlefields with milk,
they seem to emerge from wonderful forests,
   eternally virgin!

FIGURE 5. Georges Minne, *Âme de nuit*, circa 1889.

Mon âme en est triste à la fin ;
Elle est triste enfin d'être lasse,
Elle est lasse enfin d'être en vain,
Elle est triste et lasse à la fin
Et j'attends vos mains sur ma face.

J'attends vos doigts purs sur ma face,
Pareils à des anges de glace,
J'attends qu'ils m'apportent l'anneau ;
J'attends leur fraîcheur sur ma face,
Comme un trésor au fond de l'eau.

Et j'attends enfin leurs remèdes,
Pour ne pas mourir au soleil,
Mourir sans espoir au soleil !
J'attends qu'ils lavent mes yeux tièdes
Où tant de pauvres ont sommeil !

Où tant de cygnes sur la mer,
Des cygnes errants sur la mer,
Tendent en vain leur col morose !
Où, le long des jardins d'hiver,
Des malades cueillent des roses !

J'attends vos diogts purs sur ma face,
Pareils à des anges de glace,
J'attends qu'ils mouillent mes regards,
L'herbe morte de mes regards,
Où tant d'agneaux las sont épars !

My soul is sad at the end my soul
is sad to be tired at the end is sad
and tired to be in vain my soul is sad
and tired and at the end in vain
I long for your hands on my face

I long for your fingers on my face
like angels of ice your fingers on my face
I long for the ring to be brought to me
I long for their cold touch on my face
like a golden horde deep within the sea

And I long at last for their remedies
in order not to die exposed to the sun
to die in despair exposed to the sun
I long for them to bathe my eyes
where those in despair lie sleeping

Where so many swans are at sea
swans making their way over the sea
stretching in vain their sullen necks
while down in the winter gardens
there sick men are gathering roses

I long for your fingers on my face
touching my face like angels of ice
I long for them to moisten my eyes
the dead grass of my glances the fields
where so many lambs lie scattered

FIGURE 6. Georges Minne, *Untitled*, circa 1889.

Appendix: The Massacre of the Innocents

That Friday, the twenty-sixth of December, toward dinnertime, a shepherd boy came into Nazareth shrieking in terror.

Some peasants drinking beer at the Blue Lion opened the shutters overlooking the village orchard and saw a child running over the snow. They recognized Korneliz's son and called to him from the window: "What's the matter? You should be in bed!"

But he answered, trembling, that the Spaniards had come, that they had set fire to the farm and hanged his mother in the walnut grove and tied his nine little sisters to the trunk of a big tree.

The peasants rushed out of the inn, surrounded the boy and questioned him. Then he told them that the soldiers were mounted and in armor, that they had taken his uncle Petrus Krayer's cattle and would soon be in the woods with his cows and sheep.

Everyone ran to the Golden Sun, where Korneliz and his brother-in-law would be drinking their beer, and the innkeeper dashed through the village shouting that the Spaniards were coming.

Then there was a great commotion in Nazareth. The women opened their shutters, and the peasants came out of their houses with lanterns which they put out once they were in the orchard, where it was bright as day because of the snow and the full moon.

They gatherd around Korneliz and Krayer in the square, in front of the inns. Several had brought rakes and pitchforks, and they took counsel together, terror-stricken under the trees.

FIGURE 7.
Pieter Brueghel,
*The Massacre of
the Innocents*,
[1567]. Courtesy
of Kunst-
historisches
Museum, Wien.

The Massacre of the Innocents   97

But since no one knew what to do, somebody ran to get the priest, who owned Korneliz' farm. He came out of his house with the sacristan carrying the church keys. Everyone followed him into the churchyard, and he shouted to them from the top of the steeple that he could see nothing in the fields or in the woods, but that there were red clouds in the direction of his farm, although the sky was blue and full of stars over all the rest of the countryside.

Having deliberated a long time in the churchyard, they decided to hide in the woods where the Spaniards would pass and to attack them if there were not too many of them, in order to recover Petrus Krayer's cattle and the plunder taken from the farm.

The men took up their pitchforks and shovels, while the women stayed outside the church with the priest.

Looking for a good hiding-place, they got as far as the mill at the edge of the woods, and saw the farm in flames under the stars. They stopped there, in front of a frozen pond, under some huge oaks.

One shepherd, whom everyone called the Red Dwarf, climbed the hill to warn the miller, who had stopped his mill when he saw the flames on the horizon. Still, he let the shepherd in, and the two men stood at a window staring into the distance.

The moon was shining on the fire, and they saw what seemed a great host walking across the snow. When they had studied the scene for a while, the Red Dwarf came back down the hill to warn the men in the woods, and that was when they gradually made out four horsemen above the herd that seemed to be grazing on the plain.

As the peasants in their blue trousers and their red cloaks were peering toward the pond and under the trees lit by the snow, the sacristan pointed to a boxwood hedge, and the men hid behind it.

The Spaniards drove the cattle over the ice, and the sheep, having reached the hedge, were already cropping the leaves, when Korneliz pushed aside the bushes, and the others followed him with their pitchforks. Then there was a great slaughter on the ice, amid the huddled sheep and the cows that stood staring at the battle in the moonlight.

Once they had killed the horses and their riders, Korneliz dashed into the field toward the flames, while the others stripped the corpses. Then they returned to the village with their flocks. The women who were staring into the woods behind the churchyard saw them coming between the trees and ran to meet them with the priest, and they all went home together, singing and dancing in big circles, amid the children and dogs.

As they were rejoicing under the pear trees on which the Red Dwarf had hung lanterns in honor of the *kermesse*, they asked the priest what they should do next.

It was decided they would hitch up a cart and bring the nine little girls and their mother into the village. The sisters and the other members of the dead woman's family climbed into the cart, along with the priest who had difficulty walking, being old and very fat.

They returned through the woods in silence and came out on the shining plain, where they saw the naked corpses and the horses lying on the luminous ice between the trees. Then they walked toward the farm that was still burning in the middle of the plain.

When they reached the orchard and the house still red with flames, they stopped at the gate to contemplate the peasant's great disaster: his wife was hanging stark naked from the branch of a huge walnut tree, and the man himself was climbing a ladder into the tree, under which the nine little girls were awaiting their mother on the grass. He was already high in the branches when suddenly, by the light of the snow, he saw the crowd watching him. He gestured to them to help him, crying the while, and they came into the garden. Then the sacristan, the Red Dwarf, the innkeepers of the Blue Lion and the Golden Sun, the priest with a lantern, and many others climbed into the snow-laden tree in order to untie the corpse, which the village women received in their arms at the foot of the tree, as in the Descent from the Cross of Our Lord Jesus Christ.

The next day the dead woman was buried, and there were no more unusual events in Nazareth that week. But the following Sunday, starving wolves ran through the village after High Mass, and it snowed until noon; then the sun suddenly shone in the sky, and the peasants came home for dinner as was their custom and dressed for the Benediction.

There was no one to be seen in the square, for the air was bitterly cold. Only dogs and chickens wandered under the trees where some sheep were cropping a triangle of grass and the priest's housekeeper was sweeping the snow out of her garden.

Then a troop of armed men crossed the stone bridge at the far end of the village and halted in the orchard. Some peasants came out of their houses, but immediately went back inside, terrified upon recognizing the Spaniards, and stood at their windows to see what would happen next.

There were some thirty horsemen in full armor, and in the center an old man with a white beard. Behind each rider was a foot soldier in red or yellow; these dismounted and ran about over the snow to stretch their legs while several of the armed men also dismounted and pissed against the trees to which they had tied their horses.

Then they made for the Golden Sun and pounded on the door, which was reluctantly opened for them; the soldiers went inside and warmed themselves at the fire and demanded beer.

Afterwards they came out of the inn with pots and pitchers of beer and loaves of bread for their companions still ranked around the man with the white beard who was waiting among the lances.

Since the street remained empty, the leader sent horsemen behind the houses in order to keep anyone from leaving the village, and ordered the soldiers to bring to him all the children two years and under to be massacred, as it is written in the Gospel According to Saint Matthew.

They went first to the little inn of The Green Cabbage and to the nearby barber's farmhouse. One man opened the barn and a troop of hogs ran out, spreading through the village. The innkeeper and the barber came out of their houses and humbly asked the soldiers what they wanted; but these men did not understand Flemish and went inside to look for the children.

The innkeeper had a little boy who was crying, in his shirt on the table where the family had just eaten dinner. A soldier took him in his arms and carried him outside under the apple trees, while the father and mother followed in tears, beseeching him to let them have their child.

The soldiers also opened the cooper's barn, and the blacksmith's, and the cobbler's; donkeys, pigs, goats, and sheep strolled about the square. When they broke the carpenter's windows, several peasants, among them the richest and oldest in the parish, gathered in the street and walked toward the Spaniards. They respectfully removed their caps and hats in the presence of the leader in the velvet cloak, asking what he was going to do, but he too did not understand their language, and someone went to find the priest. The priest was preparing for the Benediction, putting on a golden chasuble in the sacristy. The peasant who had run to find him shouted: "The Spaniards are in the orchard!"

Alarmed, the priest ran to the church door with the choirboys who were carrying wax tapers and a censer. Then he saw the animals from the barns wandering over the snow and on the grass, the horsemen in the village, the soldiers at the doors of the houses, the horses tied to the trees along the street, and the men and women entreating the man holding the child in its shirt.

He hurried to the churchyard and the peasants turned anxiously toward their priest who had arrived between the pear trees like a god covered with gold; they surrounded him in front of the man with the white beard.

The priest spoke in Flemish and in Latin, but the leader slowly shrugged his shoulders, to show that he understood nothing.

His parishioners asked their priest in low voices: "What's he saying? What's he going to do?"

Others, seeing the priest in the orchard, timidly came out of their houses, women hurrying up to him and whispering in groups, while the soldiers who had crowded into an inn soon joined the great company that was forming in the square.

Then the man holding the innkeeper's son by one leg cut off his head with his sword.

They saw it fall in front of them, and then the rest of the body, which lay bleeding in the grass. The mother gathered it up and carried it away, forgetting the head. She ran toward her house but bumped into a tree and fell flat on her face in the snow, where she lay unconscious, while the father struggled between two soldiers.

Some young peasants threw stones and pieces of wood at the Spaniards, but the mounted men lowered their lances in unison, the women ran away, and the priest and all his parishioners began shrieking in horror among the sheep, the geese, and the dogs.

Yet as the soldiers were once more moving down the street, the townspeople fell silent, waiting to see what they were going to do next.

The troop entered the shop tended by the sacristan's sisters and then came out again quietly enough, without harming the seven women kneeling in prayer on the threshold.

From there they went to the inn of Saint Nicholas, kept by the Hunchback. Here too the doors and shutters were immediately thrown open to appease the soldiers, but they soon reappeared amid a tremendous commotion with three children in their arms, surrounded by the Hunchback, his wife, and his daughters, all beseeching the soldiers with clasped hands.

When the soldiers returned to the old man with the white beard, they set the children down at the foot of an elm where they remained sitting in the snow in their Sunday best. But one of them, wearing a yellow dress, stood up and toddled toward the sheep. A soldier chased him with a drawn sword, and the child died with his face in the grass, while the others were killed around the tree.

All the peasants and the innkeeper's daughters ran away screaming and shut themselves up in their houses. Left alone in the orchard, the priest pleaded with the Spaniards, weeping as he knelt in front of one horse after another, wringing his arms while the mother and father, sitting in the snow, wept pitiably for their dead children whom they held in their laps.

As the lancers passed down the street, they noticed a big blue farmhouse. They tried to beat down the door, but it was made of oak and studded with nails. Then they took barrels frozen in a pool in front of the door and climbed up on them in order to reach the second story, where they got in through a window.

There had been a *kermesse* here, and relatives had come to eat waffles, custard, and ham with their children. At the sound of the breaking windows they had gathered behind the table covered with pitchers and dishes. The soldiers came into the kitchen, and after a fierce struggle in which several were wounded, they seized all the little boys and girls as well as a servant who had bitten one lancer on the thumb, and came out closing the door behind them in order to keep those who were inside from following.

People in the village who had no children slowly left their houses and followed at a distance. When the soldiers reached the old man with a white beard, they flung their victims on the grass and killed them quite methodically with their lances and their swords, while men and women were crowding at the windows of the upper floor and the attic of the blue farmhouse, blaspheming and flinging their hands to heaven when they saw the red, pink, or white gowns of their children motionless on the grass between the trees. Then the soldiers hanged the servant from the half-moon sign of the inn on the other side of the street, and there was a long silence in the village.

The slaughter now became general: the mothers fled from their houses and tried to escape across the gardens and fields into the countryside, but the horsemen chased them and herded them back into the street. The peasants, caps in their clasped hands, followed on their knees the men who were dragging away their children while the dogs barked joyously amid the commotion.

The priest, arms raised to heaven, ran in front of the houses and under the trees, praying fervently, like a martyr, and the soldiers, trembling with cold, blew on their fingers as they moved up and down the street or waiting, hands in their trouser pockets and swords under their arms in front of the houses being scaled.

Seeing how timidly the peasants expressed their grief, the soldiers forced their way in groups of two or three men into the houses, and such scenes were repeated all along the street. The wife of a market-gardener who lived in an old pink-brick cottage near the church brandished a wooden stool and chased the two men carrying off her children in a wheelbarrow. When she saw them being killed, she was overcome by a sudden sickness, and someone made her sit down on the stool under a tree by the side of the road.

Other soldiers climbed up the lime trees in front of a lavender-painted farmhouse and pulled off the roof-tiles to get inside. When they came back out on the roof, the mother and father, arms outstretched, tried to follow them through the hole they had made, but the soldiers repeatedly pushed them back, finally having to strike them on the head with their swords before they could get back down to the street.

One family, shut up in the cellar of a large farmhouse, was lamenting under a grating through which the father wildly brandished a pitchfork. Outside a bald old man was sobbing all alone on a dungheap, a woman in a yellow dress had fainted on the square, and her weeping husband was pulling her up by the armpits under a pear tree; another woman in red was hugging her little girl whose hands had been cut off, and lifted one bleeding arm after the other to see whether the child would move. Another woman escaped into the countryside, and the soldiers chased after her between the haystacks, silhouetted against the snowy fields.

At the inn of the Four Sons of Aymon, a terrible siege was raging; the inhabitants had barricaded themselves inside, and the soldiers kept circling the building without managing to find a way in. Then they tried to climb up to the inn sign by the espaliers in front of the house, when they noticed a ladder behind the garden gate. They leaned it against the wall and climbed up, one after the other. But the innkeeper and his whole family hurled tables, stools, plates and cradles down on them from the windows. The ladder tipped over, and the soldiers fell.

In a wooden hut on the edge of the village, another band of soldiers found a peasant woman who was washing her children in a tub near the fire. Being old and almost completely deaf, she had not heard them come in. Two men seized the tub and carried it away, and the stupefied woman followed them with the clothes she wanted to put on her children. But when she stood on her doorstep and saw the bloodstains everywhere in the village and the swords in the orchard, the cradles lying in the street, the women kneeling and wringing their hands over the dead children, she began to scream terribly, hitting the soldiers who set down the tub in order to defend themselves. The priest ran over to them as well, wringing his hands over his chasuble, and beseeched the Spaniards in the presence of the naked children who were howling in the bathwater. Then more soldiers came and tied the mad old woman to a tree and carried off the children.

The butcher, who had hidden his little daughter, was leaning against his shopfront, watching quite indifferently. A lancer and one of the men in armor entered the house and found the child in a copper boiler. Then the butcher, in despair, took up one of his cleavers and chased them into the street, but a passing troop disarmed him and hanged him by the hands from hooks in the wall between the flayed animals, where he kicked his legs and tossed his head, blaspheming till it grew dark.

Near the churchyard there was a great crowd in front of a long farmhouse painted green. The owner was weeping bitterly on the doorstep; since he was very fat and jovial-looking, some soldiers sitting in the sun against the wall and playing with his dog listened to him sympathetically. But the soldier who had dragged away his child by one arm gestured as if to say: "What do you expect? It's not my fault!"

One peasant who was being chased jumped into a boat moored at the stone bridge and managed to escape across the pond with his wife and children. Not daring to venture out on the ice, the soldiers stumbled furiously through the reeds. They climbed into the willows on the bank, trying in vain to reach the peasants with their lances, and for a long time threatened the terrorized family in the middle of the pond.

The orchard however was still full of people, for it was here that most of the children were being slaughtered in front of the man with the white beard, who was presiding over the massacre. The little boys and girls who could walk by themselves were gathered in one place and watched the others die with great interest, munching their slices of bread and jam or clustering around the village idiot, who was playing his flute on the grass.

Then suddenly there was a concerted movement in the village. The peasants were running toward the castle built on a rise of yellow ground at one end of the street. They had glimpsed their lord leaning on the battlements of his tower, from which he was watching the massacre. Men, women, old people, hands raised, implored him as they would God in heaven, with his purple velvet mantle and his golden cap. But he raised his arms and shrugged his shoulders to indicate his helplessness, and when they beseeched him more and more intensely, kneeling in the snow and uttering terrible cries, he slowly went back into the tower, and the peasants lost all hope.

When all the children had been slaughtered, the tired soldiers dried their swords in the grass and ate their food under the pear trees. Then the lancers mounted pillion behind the soldiers in armor, and all of them left Nazareth by the stone bridge over which they had come.

The sun setting behind the woods changed the color of the village. Tired of running and pleading, the priest had flung himself down in the snow in front of the church, and his housekeeper stood beside him, staring straight ahead; they saw the street and the orchard crowded with peasants in their Sunday best wandering through the square and along the row of houses. In every doorway, the families, a dead child on the father's knees or in the mother's arms, bewailed their sorrows in amazement. Others were still lamenting their losses where they had occurred—beside a barrel, under a wheelbarrow, at the edge of a pond—or carried away the dead in silence. Several were already washing the benches, the chairs, the tables, the bloodstained shirts, and collecting the cradles flung into the street. But now almost all the mothers were mourning under the trees, bending over the dead children laid out in the grass, whom they identified by their woolen gowns.

Those who had no children strolled aimlessly around the square, sometimes stopping in front of the groups of the bereaved. The men who were not still crying went off with their dogs in pursuit of their runaway cattle, or else repaired their broken windows and gaping roofs, while the village became quite still by the light of the rising moon.